D0620468

FAR OUT FABLES

raintree
a Capstone company — publishers for children

INTRODUCING...
REX
MAMA DUCK
FIRST
SECOND
THIRD
FOURTH

MAMA DINO
THE VELOCIRAPTOR
THE FARM ANIMALS
IN...

NORTH AYRSHIRE LIBRARIES
07544278
Bertrams 25/01/2018
£4.99
B

Raintree is an imprint of Capstone Global Library Limited, a company incorporated in England and Wales having its registered office at 264 Banbury Road, Oxford, OX2 7DY – Registered company number: 6695582

www.raintree.co.uk
myorders@raintree.co.uk

Text and illustrations © Capstone Global Library Limited 2018.
The moral rights of the proprietor have been asserted.

All rights reserved. No part of this publication may be reproduced in any form or by any means (including photocopying or storing it in any medium by electronic means and whether or not transiently or incidentally to some other use of this publication) without the written permission of the copyright owner, except in accordance with the provisions of the Copyright, Designs and Patents Act 1988 or under the terms of a licence issued by the Copyright Licensing Agency, Saffron House, 6–10 Kirby Street, London EC1N 8TS (www.cla.co.uk). Applications for the copyright owner's written permission should be addressed to the publisher.

Designed by Hilary Wacholz
Edited by Abby Huff
Lettered by Jaymes Reed

ISBN 978 1 474 75029 5
21 20 19 18 17
10 9 8 7 6 5 4 3 2 1

British Library Cataloguing in Publication Data: A full catalogue record for this book is available from the British Library.

Printed and bound in China.

FAR OUT FABLES

THE UGLY DINO HATCHLING

A GRAPHIC NOVEL

BY STEPHANIE PETERS
ILLUSTRATED BY OTIS FRAMPTON

Eons ago, when dinosaurs roamed the world . . .
A velociraptor stole something very precious from a mother T-Rex.
HEH HEH! IT'S SCRAMBLED EGGS FOR BREAKFAST.
Hey, my *egg!*
YOU WANT IT? THEN COME AND GET IT!

If you insist.
WHUMP
But just when she thought her egg was safe . . .
Come to mama!
It fell into a swirling portal to another dimension in time!
Noooo!

Meanwhile, millions of years in the future . . .
POP
ZZZZZ
A sound sleeper, Mama Duck didn't notice anything strange.
TUMP
TUMP
TUMP
Until the next morning.
Well, I'll be *quacked!* I laid another egg last night.

Then she made an even more exciting discovery.
They're hatching! They're hatching!
CRICK
CRICK
CRICK
CRICK
CRICK
CRICK
Welcome, First!
I'm First!
Wait, his *name* is First?
Three guesses what she names the others.
You're *Second!*
You're *Third!*
You're *Fourth!*
And you're...
CRIIICK

Not quite what I was expecting.
POP
Mama!

That is one *seriously* ugly duckling.
Yikes!

But Fourth loved her younger brother instantly.
He's not *ugly!* He's... different.
He's different, all right.

We should call him *Rex!*
Rex?
Because it's unique. Like him.
Ooo, pretty!
Ooof!
WHUMP
What was his name again? Rex... or *Wrecks?*
Bwahaha!

At first, Rex's strangeness wasn't a big deal.
Nighty-night, my babies.
But over time . . .
Come along, my babies!
You can do it, Rex!
His differences became harder to overlook.
BLUB
BLUB
BLUB

Almost impossible, actually.
Mother, I'm tired.
Hop on, my baby!
I'm coming on board too, Mama!
Aah!
Soon, Rex's duckling brothers stopped ignoring the differences.
ROARHOROAR! HOROAR!
The chicken crossed the road to get to the other side! Get it?
Ha ha!
I don't get it.
Whoa. Turn it down, Rex!
And ignored Rex instead.
Guys? Aren't we going to play?
Pretend you can't hear him.
Hear who?
Exactly!

They don't like me because I'm so ugly.
You're not ugly. You're just *different*.
What do you mean, *different*?

Fourth tried to explain.
There's an old saying...

If it *looks* like a duckling...
Swims like a duckling...
And *quacks* like a duckling...
Quack!

Then it's a *duckling*.

Get it?
I do.
He didn't.
TA-DA! I *look* like a duckling.
I *swim* like a duckling. And listen to this...
QUROARK!
Oh, Rex.

Rex raced to show his brothers what a good duckling he was now.
Wait, Rex!
Guys, look at me. I'm just like *you!*
The boys looked – then left as fast as they could.
Guys?
Wow. How embarrassing.
Is he joking with that get-up?
Not joking – just trying *way* too hard.
That night, when the ducklings thought Rex was asleep . . .
We took a vote.
You lost.
So you have to tell Rex he doesn't fit in here.
What?!
They're right. I *don't.*

But there *must* be a place where I *do* fit in. And I'm going to *Find it!*

Fur, feathers, horns, hooves, fat, thin, tall, short. *Everyone* here is different, but no one is like me.
That's OK, though...

Ahem. Cock-a-doodle-
Because I can be like them!
ROAR!
Aaahh!
Cock-a-doodle-ROAR? What kind of wake-up call is that?

That day, Rex gave it his all.
Roar-roar-roar-roar.
Cluck-cluck-cluck-cluck.
SKKIIIRSHH
SKKIIIRSHH
Hey, I'm *strutting* here!

But Rex and the other animals just didn't mix.
Yuck. *Mud!*
Duck! Duck, goose!
Ah, mud.

Hmm... maybe I *can't* fit in here after all.
Yeah, I don't think it's working out. Sorry, Rex.

That's fine. The farm just isn't the right place for me.
I won't give up. I'll just keep looking.
Good luck, kid!
Because I have to belong *somewhere.*

And I'll find that somewhere...
If it's the *last thing* I do!
Sigh. I *really* hope this isn't the last thing I do.

Meanwhile, earlier that same day . . .
Mama, Rex has gone!
Oh, baby, Rex is a big boy.
I'm sure he'll return before dark.

But he didn't come back that night.
Where did you go, Rex?

Or the next day. Because he'd made a decision.
This is my home now.

Rex spent his days exploring the forest. He talked to many animals, but he didn't find any like him.
Days turned into weeks.

Although Rex missed his duck family . . .
Good night, Fourth.

He stayed out on his own.
Good night, Rex...*wherever* you are.

But one night, something else returned to the pond . . .

Huh? What is *that?!*

Z Z Z Z Z
Stay back, Fourth! ***The moon is on fire!***
That is neither the moon nor fire.
I'll tell you what it is – ***weird.***

The other animals came to investigate the mysterious object.
Is it dangerous?
One way to find out.

HELLO, SNACK.
Yep, it's dangerous!
ACTUALLY, FORGET THE SNACK.
I'M GOING FOR THE WHOLE BUFFET!
Aaahhh!!
Help!

Things didn't look good.
HMMM. WHO TO EAT FIRST?
But then . . .
CRASH
THUD
THUD
Could it be?
The ground is shaking! The ground is shaking!
THUD
THUD
You think?

Hey, you! Leave my family alone.
Rex!
My baby's back!
You're so big now! So strong! So...different!
Me? What about you?
What about us? A little help would be nice.

What's going on?
That jumped out of *that* and is going to eat everyone!
I don't think so.
QUROARK!
YOU LOOK FAMILIAR. HAVE WE MET?
I doubt it. I'd remember someone as ugly as you.
Ooo! *Burn!*
SKKIIIRSHH SKKIIIRSHH
See that? I taught him that move.

WHY, YOU!
Duck! Duck, Rex!
AAAHH!
SPOOSH
That should stop him!
ACK!
OR NOT.

HEH HEH. LOOKS LIKE POULTRY IS ON THE MENU TONIGHT!
Let my sister go!
YOU WANT HER? THEN COME AND GET HER!
Luckily, Rex had a trick up his sleeve.
You asked for it!
WHAP
OOF!

Gotcha!
DRAT . . . LEFT HUNGRY AGAIN.

You've grown from ugly duckling into a super *hero*, Rex!
No joke!
We were lousy brothers. Forgive us?
Where did you come up with that *awesome* tail spin?

He inherited that move – from *me!*
Rex! She looks just like you!
Is that...?

Mama?
Oh. Well, that explains a lot.
My baby!
Oh boy, oh boy! I've got a million questions.
I'll answer them all – at *home!* But you have to come now, before the portal closes.
You're leaving, aren't you?
I have to take this chance. But you're still my family too. I'll visit whenever I can!
I'll deal with *you* later.
One... two... *THREE!*

I was never a real *duckling* either. I was just...
One! Two!
You were never ugly, you know.

Me!
Three!

See you later, Rex.
So Rex was transported far away to a different place in a different time. But every now and then . . .

ROAR-HO-ROAR-HO!
No one's ever going to mess with me again. ***Hiyaa!***
He found his way back to where he first belonged.

ALL ABOUT FABLES

A fable is a short tale that teaches the reader a lesson about life, often with animal characters. At the end of a fable, there's almost always a moral (a fancy word for lesson) stated very clearly, so you don't miss it. Yes, fables can be a bit bossy. But luckily, they usually give pretty good advice. Read on to learn more about the original fable written by Danish author Hans Christian Andersen in 1843, and its moral. Can you spot any other lessons?

THE UGLY DUCKLING

One day, a swan egg rolls into a duck's nest. When all the eggs hatch, the baby swan – called a cygnet – looks a lot different from the ducklings. Although the cygnet swims better than his siblings, the farm animals tease him and call him ugly. Soon, even the mother duck says he doesn't belong. So the baby swan decides to run away. He tries living with wild ducks and then with an old lady and her pets. But he doesn't fit in. Out on his own, the cygnet nearly freezes during winter. In spring, the cygnet spots a flock of majestic swans. He worries they'll pick on him like everyone else has. But to his astonishment, they greet him with respect. Because he isn't an ugly duckling anymore. He's grown into the most beautiful swan in the entire pond.

THE MORAL

NEVER GIVE UP ON FINDING WHERE YOU BELONG
(In other words, don't change who you are to fit in – find where you're valued for being YOU!)

A FAR OUT GUIDE TO THE FABLE'S JURASSIC TWISTS!

The swan egg is swapped out for a dinosaur egg that has tumbled through a time portal!

In the original, even the mother duck and siblings teased the ugly duckling. Here, Fourth encourages Rex to stay true to himself.

The ugly duckling turns into a beautiful swan, but Rex grows up to use his awesome dino abilities to rescue the farm animals.

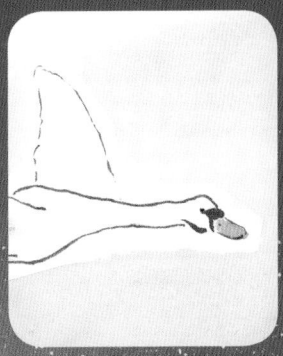

The swan leaves the ducks of the pond far behind. Rex still visits his duck family!

VISUAL QUESTIONS

The animals judge Rex because of how he looks. Do you think that's fair? Have you ever felt like you don't fit in? Talk about your answers.

The background in this panel is orange and yellow. Why do you think the illustrator chose to do this? What feeling does it create?

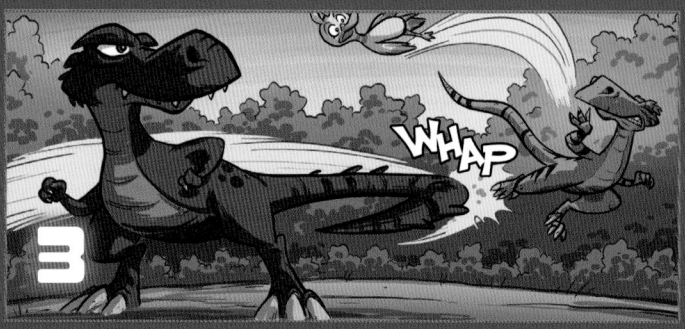

Rex is teased for being different, but his differences help to save the day. In your own words, discuss how Rex uses his unique dinosaur abilities to defeat the velociraptor.

List three ways Rex tries to fit in with the ducklings and farm animals. Did you think his plans would work? Why or why not?

What is making the "Thud" sounds in the forest? How do you know that? Look back at page 26 if you need help.

The art in graphic novels can tell you a lot about what a character is feeling or thinking. How do you think Rex feels here? Use examples from the art and text to support your answer.

AUTHOR

Stephanie Peters worked as a children's book editor for ten years before she started writing books herself. She has since written forty books, including *Sleeping Beauty*, *Magic Master* and the New York Times best-seller *A Princess Primer: A Fairy Godmother's Guide to Being a Princess*. When not at her computer, Peters enjoys playing with her two children, going to the gym or working on home improvement projects with her patient and supportive husband, Daniel.

ILLUSTRATOR

Otis Frampton is a writer and artist. He is the creator of *Oddly Normal*, published by Image Comics. He is also one of the artists on the popular animated web series *How It Should Have Ended*.

GLOSSARY

decision act of making up your mind about what to do

eon long period of time that can't be measured

explore travel through a new area in order to learn or for adventure

familiar well known or easily recognized; if something *seems* familiar, you're not quite sure if you know it and can't fully remember

inherit receive something from a parent, such as looks, habits or skills

insist demand or ask in a very firm way

overlook ignore or not pay attention to something

portal large, impressive opening or entrance

poultry birds raised for their eggs and meat; chickens, turkeys, ducks and geese are poultry

precious having great importance or value

strut walk in a proud way

unique one of a kind and unlike anything else

wreck destroy or damage in a violent way

THE MORAL OF THE STORY IS... EPIC!

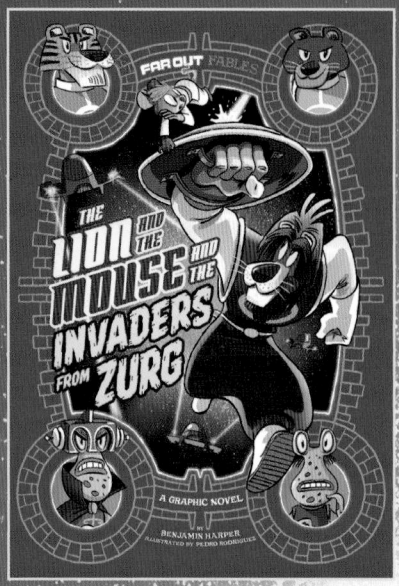

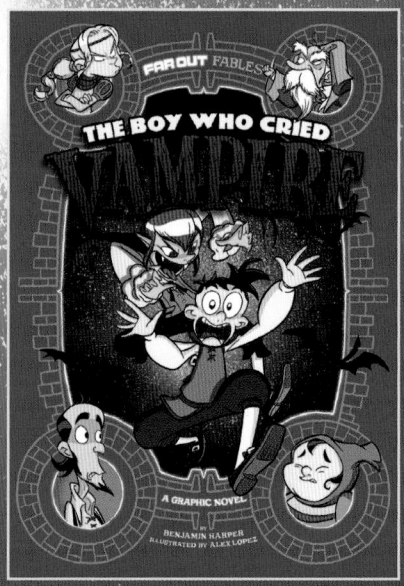

FAR OUT FABLES